The Big Book About Jesus

Mark Water

Illustrated by
Graham Round

THOMAS NELSON PUBLISHERS
Nashville • Atlanta • London • Vancouver

Published in Nashville, Tennessee, by Thomas Nelson, Inc., Publishers and distributed in Canada by Word Communications, Ltd, Richmond, British Columbia.

The Bible version used in this publication is THE NEW KING JAMES VERSION. Copyright © 1979, 1980, 1982, 1990, Thomas Nelson, Inc., Publishers.

Printed in Malaysia.

Library of Congress Cataloging-in-Publication Data

Water, Mark.
    The Big Book About Jesus / Mark Water ; illustrated by Graham Round. — US ed.
        p.   cm.
    ISBN 0-7852-7892-3 (hard cover)
    1. Jesus Christ—Biography—Juvenile literature.
2. Second Advent—Juvenile literature.   3. Church history—Primitive and early church, ca. 30-600—Juvenile literature.   [1. Jesus Christ–Biography. 2. Bible—N.T.]
1. Round, Graham, ill.   11. Title.
BT302.P55 1995
232.9'01—dc20
    [B]   94-38518
                                                CIP
                                                AC

1 2 3 4 5 6 — 00 99 98 97 96 95

CONTENTS

1 PROPHECIES ABOUT JESUS

Bethlehem for His birth

Tucked away in an Old Testament book is God's promise that a ruler will come from Bethlehem: "Bethlehem Ephrathah, you are one of the smallest towns in Judah, but out of you I will bring a ruler." Who could have predicted that anyone important would be born in such a tiny village? (See Micah 5:2.)

Born of a virgin

So many things about Jesus were plain impossible! For starters, His birth was miraculous. Isaiah the prophet had said, "A virgin will become pregnant and have a Son, and He will be called Immanuel." (See Isaiah 7:14; Matthew 1:23.)

Out of Egypt

It was the most terrible happening. All the baby boys two years old and younger were killed by King Herod's soldiers. Joseph had escaped to Egypt one night with Mary and the baby Jesus. As Matthew records it, "This was done to make what the Lord had said through the prophet come true, 'I called My Son out of Egypt.'" (See Matthew 2:15; Hosea 11:1.)

Descended from David

Everyone knew that David was Israel's greatest king. The prophet Isaiah went one better. He predicted that there would be a future king who would be called "Wonderful, Counselor, Mighty God, Prince of Peace." He would rule as King David's successor. The angel Gabriel told Mary that her baby would be this person.
(See Luke 1:32; Isaiah 9:6–7.)

Christ will suffer

There are so many prophecies in the Old Testament which tell us about Jesus. Lots of them say that He would not just heal people and preach to people, but that He would also suffer. Until Jesus died on the cross no one really understood these words from the prophet Isaiah: "Because of our sins He was wounded. He was beaten because of the evil we did."
(See Isaiah 53:5–6.)

Christ will heal the blind

One day, Jesus went into the synagogue in Nazareth and read these words: "The Spirit of the LORD is upon Me, because He has chosen Me to bring good news to the poor. He has sent Me to proclaim liberty to the captives and recovery of sight to the blind." All eyes were on Jesus. He rolled up the scroll, gave it back to the attendant, sat down, and said, "This passage of Scripture has come true today, as you heard it being read." (See Luke 4:16–21; Isaiah 61:1–2.)

2 THE FIRST CHRISTMAS

Angels

Angels were kept busy on the first Christmas. The English word *angel* comes from the Greek word *angelos*, which means "messenger." Sometimes angels are disguised as ordinary people. Sometimes they wear dazzling white clothes. Jesus said that guardian angels look after children.
(See Matthew 18:10.)

An angel and the teenager

The angel who spoke to Mary was called Gabriel. When the angel came, Mary was engaged to Joseph. She was probably about 14 or 15 years old. In those days girls married when they were very young. An engagement was treated very seriously. If you wanted to break off an engagement you had to sign papers and get a divorce.
(See Luke 1:26–27.)

Gabriel's surprising news

The angel Gabriel told Mary that she was going to have a baby. Her baby would be a very great king. He did not have a human father. His Father was God. The angel said, "Nothing is impossible with God." Mary was very happy. She sang a song of praise to God. We call her song "The Magnificat."
(See Luke 1:29–38 and 46–55.)

A dream

Mary was engaged to a carpenter named Joseph. Joseph was upset when he found out that Mary was pregnant and didn't want to marry her. God spoke to him in a dream. God said, "The baby is born by the power of the Holy Spirit. You must call Him Jesus." The word *Jesus* means "God saves." Joseph married Mary at once.
(See Matthew 1:19–21.)

The great count

Mary and Joseph lived in the town of Nazareth in Palestine. Their country was occupied by the Romans. The Roman emperor, who was Caesar Augustus, wanted to count everybody who lived in his empire. The count, called a census, took place in 5 B.C. All the people had to go back to their hometowns and enter their names in a register. Joseph had to go to Bethlehem in Judea.
(See Luke 2:1–5.)

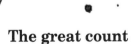

A bumpy journey

It was 90 miles from Nazareth to Bethlehem. There were no cars in those days! All the ordinary people traveled by donkey. The journey probably took at least three days.
(See Luke 2:4–5.)

No room

Bethlehem was the town where King David had been born hundreds of years before. This story was first written in Greek. The Greek word we have translated as *inn* means "temporary shelter." The Romans used to put up big tents for all the extra travelers. The tent at Bethlehem was full. The Bible does not say Jesus was born in a stable. But we guess He was because a "manger" is an animal's feeding trough.
(See Luke 2:6–7.)

Songs in the night

Shepherds did not stay out all night in winter. So Jesus was probably not born in December. Respectable people looked down on shepherds. When a new king was born in a palace, music was always played. The angels provided the music for the King of heaven.
(See Luke 2:8–21.)

The wise men

The "wise men" were probably not kings but "students of the stars." They did not follow the star all the way from their home in the East. They only saw it at its rising. They went to Jerusalem because they expected a new king to be born in a palace. The star came back when they left Jerusalem. The Bible does not say how many "wise men" there were. We guess there were three because there were three gifts—gold, frankincense, and myrrh. The wise men did not go to a stable, but a house. So Mary and Joseph may have stayed a while in Bethlehem.
(See Matthew 2:1–12.)

3 FAMILY LIFE WITH JESUS

The baby Jesus makes Simeon smile

Everyone loves to look at tiny babies, touch their tiny fingers, and maybe hold them in their arms. But when the gray-bearded Simeon saw the 40-day-old baby Jesus in the temple, he didn't just take Jesus in his arms because he loved babies. Simeon "gave thanks to God," because "with my eyes I have seen Your salvation." And yet, all he had seen was a baby! (See Luke 2:22–32.)

The 84-year-old Anna sees the baby Jesus

Mary and Joseph did not know what to make of Simeon's speech about Jesus. Then they bumped into someone else in the temple—a very old woman called Anna. Anna made Mary and Joseph scratch their heads even more, because Anna "spoke about the Child to all who were waiting for God to set Jerusalem free." (See Luke 2:36–38.)

King Herod goes on a rampage

When Jesus was born, not everyone rushed to worship Him and love Him. His cradle was a manger, and before He could walk, King Herod wanted to have Him killed! Herod could not bear the thought that a "king" had been born in Bethlehem as the "wise men" had told him. So he killed all the baby boys. (See Matthew 2:16–18.)

Jesus' family escape as refugees to Egypt

It was just as well that Joseph took notice of his dreams. God had told him in his latest dream to "get up, take the Child and His mother and escape to Egypt, and stay there until I tell you to leave." Jesus became a refugee. (See Matthew 2:13–15.)

Another dream for Joseph

After Herod died, "an angel of the Lord appeared in a dream to Joseph in Egypt and said, 'Get up, take the young Child and His mother, and go to the land of Israel, because those who tried to kill the Child are dead.'" So they gave their donkey a specially big breakfast and set out for Israel. Joseph heard that Archelaus, who cruelly killed 3,000 Jews, was now king, and so he was afraid. An angel told Joseph not to return to Bethlehem in Judea but to go away from the new king, to Nazareth in Galilee. (See Matthew 2:19–23.)

A visit to the big city
It was such an exciting time of the year. Time to go up to the big city of Jerusalem. They did it at the same time every year. They always timed it so that they arrived in time for the Passover festival. It was the time the Jews remembered how God had rescued them from Egypt and was as big a festival as our Christmas and Easter.
(See Luke 2:41–42.)

The 12-year-old Jesus talks in the temple
Many teenagers would have gone somewhere to have fun. But not Jesus. Although He was only 12 years old He was sitting with the Jewish teachers in the temple, listening to them and asking them questions. "All who heard Him were amazed at His intelligent answers."
(See Luke 2:43–52.)

Jesus as a carpenter
There is an 18-year silence about Jesus. There's nothing recorded about Him between the time He was a 12-year-old boy in the temple to the time He was a 30-year-old man. As Joseph was a carpenter everyone assumes that Jesus became a carpenter too.
(See Matthew 13:55.)

4 JESUS CHANGES JOBS

Jesus stops being a carpenter

If Jesus did work as a carpenter in the family business He changed jobs when He was 30 years old. Jesus was killed when He was 33. So He was a traveling preacher for only three years. Luke clearly thought that those were the most important years of His life as he says that when Jesus was 30 "He began His work." (See Luke 3:23.)

A dove

As Jesus was baptized by John in the river Jordan, two very strange things happened. "The heaven was opened to Jesus, and He saw the Spirit of God coming down like a dove and alighting upon Him." (See Matthew 3:16.)

With cousin John in the water

John the Baptist, Jesus' cousin, was the most outspoken preacher imaginable. He called some of his congregation "vipers" as they came to hear him preaching in the open air around the River Jordan. But John was lost for words when Jesus asked him to baptize Him. After John protested, "I ought to be baptized by You," he went ahead and did baptize Jesus. (See Matthew 3:1–15 and Luke 3:1–22.)

A voice

As if the dove at Jesus' baptism wasn't enough, "A voice said from heaven, 'This is My own dear Son, with whom I am pleased.'" So there it was. Jesus was no ordinary "carpenter's son"; He was the Son of God. (See Matthew 3:17.)

Getting the Jesus team together

Jesus was no loner. He took the business of choosing His twelve-man team very seriously. He spent one whole night praying before He made His selection.
(See Luke 6:12–16.)

Four fishermen who followed Jesus

Jesus invited Andrew and his brother Peter to follow Him. He said they would no longer be catching fish but people: "Come with Me and I will teach you to catch people." Then Jesus invited two more brothers to follow Him, James and John. The tough fishermen became Jesus' closest and most trusted followers.
(See Matthew 4:18–22.)

Jesus' family tree, back to Adam

Matthew starts off his gospel by tracing Jesus' ancestors back to Abraham. Luke goes even further back to Adam. From what may appear to be boring lists of names to us, Matthew and Luke are saying to their readers, Take note—Jesus is special.
(See Matthew 1:1–17; Luke 3:23–38.)

ABRAHAM to DAVID
Abraham
Isaac
Jacob
Judah
. . . . . .
Boaz
Obed
Jesse
David

DAVID to JECONIAH
David
Solomon
Rehoboam
Abijah
. . . .
Josiah
Jeconiah

JECONIAH to JESUS
Jeconiah
Shealtiel
Zerubbabel
. . . .
Matthan
Jacob
Joseph
(the husband of Mary)
Jesus

5 PEOPLE JESUS LIKED

Children the disciples had no time for

Lots of the people Jesus liked, other people had no time for. Jesus' disciples had no time for kids. They just wanted to tell them to "clear out." In fact, once, some people brought children to Jesus, for Him to bless, and the disciples "scolded them." This made Jesus angry and He said, "Let the children come to Me, and do not stop them; because the kingdom of God belongs to such as these."
(See Mark 10:13–16.)

Cousin John and his courage

Poor cousin John. He was in a dark, damp, dingy prison. He longed for freedom and for fresh air. He sent a messenger to ask Jesus, "Are You really the Christ?" Jesus said, "Tell John what you see. The blind can see, the lame can walk...and the good news is preached to the poor." Then Jesus told the crowd, "John the Baptist is greater than any man who has ever lived."
(See Matthew 11:1–15.)

A Roman soldier

He knew what it was to give orders: "Do this! March there! Come here!" This crack Roman soldier said to Jesus, "Just give the word, Jesus, and I know my very ill servant will be healed." Jesus could hardly believe His ears. This non-Jewish soldier had such complete faith in Him. Jesus told him, "Go home, and what you believe will be done for you." His servant was cured that very hour. (See Matthew 8:5–13.)

Peter, getting it right

"Who do you say I am?" Jesus asked, putting His disciples on the spot. Lots of ideas were flying around. Some people said He was John the Baptist, some Elijah, some Jeremiah. Peter had no doubt who Jesus was. "You are the Messiah, the Son of the living God." "Yes, Peter, you're right," said Jesus, "and only My Father in heaven told you this."
(See Matthew 16:13–20.)

Lazarus

It says in the Bible that Jesus loved Lazarus, as well as his two sisters, Mary and Martha. You might have thought that Jesus would have loved Mary because she did what was best, and not loved Martha, but John says, "Jesus loved Martha and her sister and Lazarus."
(See John 11:5.)

Mary, who loved to listen to Jesus

Jesus often stayed with Lazarus and his two sisters, Mary and Martha. Jesus loved each of them. Mary's greatest delight was sitting at Jesus' feet and listening to His every word.
(See Luke 10:38–39.)

Martha, too busy for words

Martha, the sister of Lazarus and Mary, once complained to Jesus, "Lord, don't You care that my sister has left me to do all the work myself?" Jesus replied, "Martha, Martha! you are worried and troubled over so many things. But just one thing is needed. Mary has chosen the right thing…"
(See Luke 10:40–42.)

6 PEOPLE JESUS SCOLDED

People who did not do what they said

Jesus loved everyone, but He always reproved people for doing evil and wrong things. Jesus had no time for people who were full of talk but had no matching actions. He once said, "Not everyone who says to Me, 'Lord, Lord,' shall enter the kingdom of heaven, but he who does the will of My Father in heaven." (See Matthew 7:21–27.)

The man Jesus called a fox

Yes, Jesus did once call the ruler Herod a fox. He told the Pharisees: "Go, tell that fox, 'Behold, I cast out demons.'" Herod was also called "sly" and "a wily sneak" by other people. Everybody, including Jesus, knew how cunning Herod was. (See Luke 13:31–33.)

The Sadducees for their stupid question

The Sadducees told Jesus a story about a woman who had married seven brothers. She married the first brother, and he died; so she married the second brother, and he died; and so on. Then came their question to Jesus. "In the resurrection [which the Sadducees did not even believe in] whose wife will she be?" Jesus replied, "Nobody's! When the dead rise to life, they will be like the angels of God in heaven and will not marry." (See Matthew 22:23–33.)

The show-offs (teachers of the Law)

Watch out, Jesus warned a large crowd, for the teachers of the Law, who like to walk around in their long robes and be greeted with respect in the marketplace, who choose the best seats in the synagogues and the best places at feasts. They do everything so that people will see them! (See Mark 12:38–40.)

The Pharisees: outwardly clean, inwardly dirty

Jesus was eating a meal as a guest of a Pharisee. The Pharisees were surprised when they noticed that Jesus had not washed before eating. Jesus did not mince His words in His reply to them: "You are really good at giving to God one-tenth of the plants from your herb garden. But you are really bad when it comes to justice and love for God." (See Luke 11:37–44.)

The people Jesus called snakes

Yes, Jesus once called a group of people "snakes." It was some of those Pharisees again—top religious leaders at the bottom of the league of love for and trust in Jesus. Jesus had just wonderfully healed a man who was blind and could not speak. The Pharisees called Jesus the devil! Jesus replied, "You snakes! How can you say good things when you are evil?" (See Matthew 12:22–37.)

People who upset the faith of children

Millstones were used in mills to grind up the grain. They were so heavy that two or three men could hardly lift them. Jesus said that people who upset the faith of children would be better off to have a millstone hung around the neck and then be thrown into the sea to drown. (See Matthew 18:1–7.)

7 JESUS IS PUT ON THE SPOT

The emperor or God?

The Pharisees laid a trap for Jesus. They asked Him this trick question: "Is it against our law to pay taxes to the Roman emperor or not?" Jesus saw the trap. If He said, "Do not pay taxes to the emperor," He would be accused of breaking one law. And if He said, "Do pay these taxes," He would be accused of breaking another law. So Jesus said, "Pay the emperor what belongs to the emperor, and pay God what belongs to God."
(See Matthew 22:15–22.)

Plucking grain on the Sabbath

"Caught you! Why are Your disciples breaking the law by harvesting grain on the Sabbath?" the Pharisees demanded. Jesus replied with one of His remarkable sayings: "The Sabbath was made for man, and not man for the Sabbath. Therefore the Son of Man is also Lord of the Sabbath."
(See Mark 2:23–28.)

Wasting expensive perfume

"What a waste," complained Judas Iscariot. "All that expensive perfume that Mary has poured over Jesus' feet. Well, we could have sold the perfume and given the money to the poor." "Do not criticize Mary," replied Jesus. "You always have the poor, but you do not always have Me."
(See John 12:1–8.)

Do you pay tax?

Peter told Jesus, "They are asking us to pay the temple tax." Jesus said to Peter, "Go fish." The first fish Peter caught had a coin in its mouth, exactly enough to pay their temple tax!
(See Matthew 17:24–27.)

Wash your hands!

The goodie-goodie Pharisees thought they had caught Jesus. "Why do Your disciples not walk according to the tradition of the elders, but eat bread with unwashed hands?" they accused. *This must make Your disciples unclean*, they thought. The Pharisees didn't eat unless they washed their hands in a special way. They even washed their cups, bowls, and jugs in a special way as well, so everybody would think how holy they were. Jesus replied, "Whatever enters a man from outside cannot defile him.... For from within, out of the heart of men, proceed evil thoughts...thefts...foolishness. All these things come from within and defile a man." (See Mark 7:1–23.)

Show us a sign

"Give us a miracle. Show us a sign. Then we will believe," lied some of the Pharisees. Jesus' reply left them in no doubt about what He thought of their phoney request: "No sign shall be given to these people." (See Mark 8:11–13.)

He is just the carpenter's son

When Jesus returned as a preacher and healer to His hometown of Nazareth, the people did not welcome Him. They criticized Him by saying, "He is just the son of the carpenter." They were so against Jesus that Jesus said to them, "A prophet is not without honor except in his own country and in his own family." Because they had so little faith Jesus did not perform many miracles there. (See Matthew 13:53–58.)

8 JESUS' FAMOUS SAYINGS

A saying for people who need God
These eight beatitudes of Jesus are probably His most famous sayings. Jesus said people who knew they needed God would be happy: "Happy are those who know they are spiritually poor; the kingdom of heaven belongs to them!" (See Matthew 5:3.)

A saying for people who are humble
Humble people were never meant to go around being hangdog down-in-the-mouths: "Happy are those who are humble; they will receive what God has promised!" (See Matthew 5:5.)

A saying for people who do right
"Me first, my neighbor next, and God last" is a popular motto. Jesus reversed it and said, "Happy are those whose greatest desire is to do what God requires; God will satisfy them fully!" (See Matthew 5:6.)

A saying for people who are sad
If you cry over your sins and weep buckets of tears over your bad ways you will be happy: "Happy are those who mourn; God will comfort them!" (See Matthew 5:4.)

A saying for people who show mercy

Here is a promise from Jesus. It is for everyone who is kind and merciful toward other people: "Happy are those who are merciful to others; God will be merciful to them!" (See Matthew 5:7.)

A saying for people who are pure in heart

If you could wish for anything in the world it would not be better than the reward Jesus promises the pure in heart: "Happy are the pure in heart; they will see God!" (See Matthew 5:8.)

A saying for people who bring peace

There is war everywhere: between nations, between families, between moms and dads, and between kids and parents. Jesus' message to our war-torn world is "work for peace." "Happy are the peacemakers; God will call them His children!" (See Matthew 5:9.)

A saying for people who are treated badly for doing good

What do Jesus Christ, the apostle Peter, Stephen, and the apostle John have in common? They were all mistreated for their faith in God. Jesus said, "Happy are those who are mistreated because they do what God requires; the kingdom of heaven belongs to them!" (See Matthew 5:10.)

9 THREE STORIES JESUS TOLD

The farmer and the seed

The seed stands for God's Word, the Bible. It is scattered on four types of soil. Each soil stands for a different type of person.

Soil No. 1

This soil is a path. "Gobble, gobble, gobble. Thanks for breakfast, lunch, and dinner," twitter the pecking birds. Person No. 1 has God's Word snatched away by the devil before it can take root.

Soil No. 2

This is rocky ground. "Help, there is not enough to drink. I need water," says the seed. Person No. 2 starts to grow but is knocked out as soon as Mr. Mistreatment comes along.

Soil No. 3

This soil is full of thornbushes. "These bushes will be the death of me. They are not giving me room to breathe," cries the seed. Person No. 3 starts to grow but is choked to death by worry, riches, and the pleasures of life.

Soil No. 4

This is the good soil. Each seed produces 100 grains. Now, that is not a 100 percent increase, but more like a 100,000 percent increase! Person No. 4 "hears the word, keeps it with a noble and good heart, persists, and bears fruit." (See Luke 8:4–8, 11–15.)

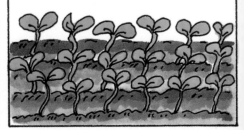

The Pharisee and . . .

Here is a parable for people who were sure of their own goodness and despised everyone else. It starts with a picture of a Pharisee congratulating himself on how good he is: "I fast twice a week. I give away 10 percent of my income. I am just so good. I am not like any of those greedy, dishonest people I could mention . . . like that dreadful tax collector over there."

. . . the tax collector

All the tax collector would say is, "God, be merciful to me a sinner!" No prizes for guessing who was the hero in Jesus' eyes! "I tell you the tax collector, and not the Pharisee, was in the right with God when he went home. For everyone who makes himself great will be humbled, and everyone who humbles himself will be made great." (See Luke 18:9–14.)

The man who was mugged

In this story two religious men left an injured man to die. The hero was a foreigner, and today we call him the good Samaritan. (See Luke 10:25–37.)

10 JESUS AND THE SCRIPTURES

How Jesus used the Scriptures when under attack

Three times the devil tried to trip Jesus up with temptations in the desert. Three times Jesus quoted verses from the Old Testament. Each time Jesus introduced the quotations with the words, "It is written."
(See Matthew 4:1–11.)

Jesus taught a lesson from Noah

Jesus said that in Noah's day, everybody kept on eating and drinking "until the day that Noah entered the ark, and the flood came and destroyed them all."
(See Luke 17:26–27.)

Jesus taught a lesson from Abraham

Jesus taught a lesson about "back to the future." The Pharisees could not believe that Jesus knew Abraham. "I am telling you the truth," Jesus said. "Before Abraham was born, 'I AM.'" They got the message. Jesus was saying He was God.
(See John 8:48–59.)

Jesus taught a lesson from Moses

Jesus said, "As Moses lifted up a bronze snake on a pole in the wilderness, even so must the Son of Man be lifted up." Moses put the bronze snake where people could see it. They could turn to it and ask God to forgive them. "In the same way," said Jesus, "the Son of Man must be lifted up so that everyone who believes in Him may have eternal life."
(See John 3:14–17.)

Jesus taught a lesson from Jonah

Jesus used Jonah's three-day stay inside a huge fish as a picture of His own death and resurrection. After His death He would rise again "on the third day," as the Bible says.
(See Matthew 12:38–41.)

Jesus taught a lesson from Lot's wife

Jesus was teaching that God's kingdom will come when people least expect it. So, Jesus said, "Remember Lot's wife!" She looked back at the cities of Gomorrah and Sodom as God destroyed them. She ended up as a pillar of salt! (See Luke 17:31–37.)

Jesus taught a lesson from Solomon

"STOP worrying! Do not worry about the clothes or shoes you do not have." How could Jesus get that message across? He used King Solomon. Jesus said, "Why worry about clothes? Look at how the wildflowers grow; they do not work or make clothes for themselves. And yet I say to you that not even Solomon with all his wealth had clothes as beautiful as one of these flowers. God clothes the wild grass. Will He not much more clothe you?" (See Matthew 6:28–30.)

11 JESUS—THE GREATEST STORYTELLER

The story about the two men who owed money
Scene 1: The king's courtroom

A servant owed a king an impossible debt—like a million dollars! "Pay me all you owe," demanded the king. "What? You cannot pay me back? You, your wife, and your kids are to be sold as slaves." The servant fell on his knees and begged, "Be patient." The king's heart was touched and he canceled the complete debt.

Scene 2: Outside the palace

The servant who had just been forgiven bumped into a fellow servant. "You owe me some money. [It was only a few dollars.] Give it to me now, or I will choke you." The second servant begged, "Be patient." The first servant's heart was untouched. "I will throw you into prison, until you pay."

Scene 3: Back in the king's courtroom

Other servants saw all that went on. They were very upset and reported to the king. You can feel the king's anger as he said to the first servant, "You wicked servant! I forgave you all that debt because you begged me. You should have had mercy on your fellow servant, just as I had pity on you."

Punch line time

All of Jesus' parables had one key lesson to teach. It was often summed up in a punch line. Thinking of the fate of the unforgiving servant, Jesus rounded this parable off with the words: "So My heavenly Father also will do to you if each of you, from his heart, does not forgive his brother."
(See Matthew 18:21–35.)

The story of the sheep and the goats
Setting the scene:
The scene is Judgment Day, with the King (God) in charge. He is like a shepherd as He separates the sheep from the goats. The sheep are the righteous people who go to His right side, and the goats go to the left.

The righteous (the sheep)
The King says to the people on His right, "Come, you blessed of My Father! Come and possess the kingdom that has been prepared for you. I was hungry and you gave Me food; I was thirsty and you gave Me drink; I was a stranger and you took Me in; I was naked and you clothed Me; I was sick and you visited Me; I was in prison and you came to Me." The righteous are surprised and puzzled: "Lord, when did we see You hungry and feed You, or thirsty and give You drink, and so on?"

The first punch line
The King answers, "I say to you, whenever you did it to one of the least important of My brothers, you did it to Me!"

The others (the goats)
Then the King says to those on His left, "Get away from Me, you that are under God's curse. I was hungry and you gave Me no food; I was thirsty and you gave Me no drink"; and so on. The goats were surprised and indignant: "Lord, when did we see You hungry or thirsty or a stranger or naked or sick or in prison, and did not help You?"

The second punch line
The King replies, "I say to you, whenever you refused to help one of the least important of these, you refused to help Me."
(See Matthew 25:31–46.)

12 COMMANDS OF JESUS

"Go, wash"
"Go, wash in the pool of Siloam," Jesus ordered a man who had been born blind. The man went, washed his face, and came back seeing.
(See John 9:1–12.)

"Do not make a big show"
Jesus said, "When you give something to a needy person, do not make a big show of it as the phonies do in the houses of worship and in the streets. But when you help a needy person, do it in such a way that even your closest friend will not know about it."
(See Matthew 6:2–3.)

"Heal the sick"
Jesus sent out 36 pairs of men (72 men in all). When they arrived in a town, as well as healing the sick, they had to say, "The kingdom of God has come near to you."
(See Luke 10:1–12.)

"Take the plank out of your eye"

Jesus was telling people not to judge others: "Why do you look for the speck in your brother's eye, but pay no attention to the plank in your own eye? How can you say to your brother, 'Let me take that speck out of your eye,' yet cannot even see the plank in your own eye? Hypocrite! First take the plank out of your own eye, and then you will see clearly to remove the speck that is in your brother's eye."
(See Luke 6:37–42.)

"Pray in secret"

Jesus said, "When you pray, do not be like the hypocrites. They love to pray standing on the street corners, so that everyone will see them. But when you pray, go into your room, close the door, and pray to your Father, who is unseen."
(See Matthew 6:5–6.)

"Stand up"

Four friends had made a hole in the roof of the house where Jesus was teaching. Through the hole they gently lowered their paralyzed friend. Jesus said two things: (1) "Your sins are forgiven," and (2) "Get up, pick up your mat, and go home."
(See Mark 2:1–12.)

"Love your enemies"

We expect Jesus to say, "Love God," and "Love your neighbors." But it shocks us when He says, "Love your enemies, and pray for those who spitefully use you."
(See Matthew 5:43–48.)

13 MANY MIRACLES

The day the wine ran out at the party

The wedding party at Cana nearly spluttered to a halt. No more wine. There were six stone waterpots. Jesus said, "Fill them up to the brim with water." He turned the water into wine on a grand scale. Each waterpot held 100 liters; each liter filled 7 wine glasses = 4,200 glasses of wine!
(See John 2:1–12.)

The son who came alive again on the way to his funeral

What a surprise the widow of Nain had about her only son! What a surprise the young man had! He was in his coffin, on his way to be buried, when Jesus brought him back to life.
(See Luke 7:11–17.)

Over 5,000 people are fed by Jesus

Jesus was given only two fish and five loaves of bread. Yet 5,000 men, not to mention the women and children, all had enough to eat. And the leftovers filled 12 baskets.
(See Matthew 14:13–21.)

Jesus heals many people

It was busier than a doctor's waiting room. A large crowd of people came to Jesus. They all walked very slowly because they carried or helped along friends or relatives who were sick. There were people who could not see and people who could not walk. "They placed them at Jesus' feet, and He healed them." (See Matthew 15:29–31.)

Nets full of fish

They had caught nothing, not even a small fish, all night long. Jesus told Peter to let his nets down in the deep water. Peter and Andrew caught so many fish, they called James and John to help them. Their nets were at the breaking point. They filled both boats with fish and nearly sank them in the process.
(See Luke 5:1–11.)

Jesus walks on water

The disciples were in a boat that was being "tossed by the waves because the wind was blowing against it." Then they saw Jesus on the water. No wonder they thought it was a ghost at that time of the morning, between 3:00 A.M. and 6:00 A.M. When Jesus climbed into the boat, they thought differently. "Truly You are the Son of God!" they exclaimed.
(See Matthew 14:22–33.)

Complete calm after a terrible storm

It was okay for Jesus. He was fast asleep in the stern, with His head on a pillow. The disciples were terrified as they watched the big waves break over the bow of the boat, almost sinking them. They woke Jesus up. To the wind, Jesus said, "Be quiet!" To the waves, Jesus said, "Be still!" The disciples' reaction? "Who can this be, that even the wind and the waves obey Him!" (See Mark 4:35–41.)

14 JESUS AND HIS FIRST FOLLOWERS

The day three were dazzled by Jesus

Peter, James, and John were dazzled. As Jesus prayed, His face changed, and so did His clothes. They shone a dazzling white. Then two people, Elijah and Moses, "appeared in glory." They talked about how Jesus would soon fulfill God's purpose by dying in Jerusalem. (See Luke 9:28–36.)

The day James and John's mother asked a wrong question

James and John's mother came to Jesus with her sons and asked a favor: "Promise me that these two sons of mine will sit at Your right and Your left when You are King." Jesus could not say "yes" because "the places belong to those for whom it is prepared by My Father." The other 10 disciples were furious with James and John. Jesus told them all, "Whoever desires to be first among you, let him be your servant." (See Matthew 20:20–28.)

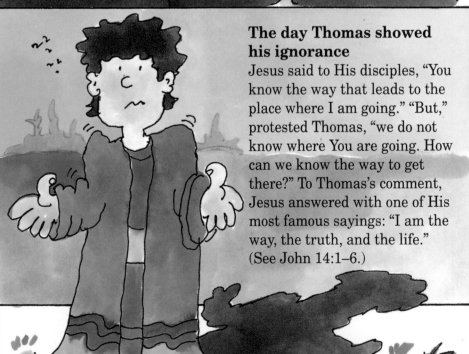

The day Thomas showed his ignorance

Jesus said to His disciples, "You know the way that leads to the place where I am going." "But," protested Thomas, "we do not know where You are going. How can we know the way to get there?" To Thomas's comment, Jesus answered with one of His most famous sayings: "I am the way, the truth, and the life." (See John 14:1–6.)

The day Peter sank on the water

Have you ever had a sinking feeling? It happened to Peter. There he was, walking on the water toward Jesus. All was fine until Peter concentrated on the strong wind and became scared. He had taken his eyes off Jesus, and he began to sink. He cried out. Jesus stretched out His hand and grabbed Peter. (See Matthew 14:22–32.)

The day Jesus spoke about a camel and a needle

Jesus wanted to explain how hard it is for rich people to be His followers. He said, "It is much harder for a rich person to enter the kingdom of God than for a camel to go through the eye of a needle." But it is impossible for a camel to be threaded through a needle's eye! Exactly. You see the point! (See Luke 18:18–30.)

The day Jesus told Peter to forgive 490 times

Forgiving people is hard. Peter knew that. So he asked Jesus, "Lord, if my brother keeps on sinning against me, how many times do I have to forgive him? Up to seven times?" Peter probably thought, *Yes, seven times is most generous.* Jesus gave a reply Peter had not bargained for: "No, not up to seven times, but up to seventy times seven." In other words, never stop forgiving! (See Matthew 18:21–23.)

The day Judas asked a question he knew the answer to

You could have heard a pin drop when Jesus said, "One of you will betray Me." Judas asked, "Surely, Teacher, You do not mean me?"—as if he did not know all along. He had just made a deal to betray Jesus for 30 silver coins. (See Matthew 26:17–25.)

15 JESUS VERSUS THE DEVIL

Three devilish attacks on Jesus

Jesus was preparing Himself in the desert to start His work—preaching, teaching, and healing—when the devil tempted Jesus three times.

Temptation No. 1

"Go on, Jesus," egged on the devil, "turn these stones into bread. You must be starving."

Temptation No. 2

"Go on, Jesus, throw Yourself off the top of the temple. Go on, I know You can do it. The angels will keep You safe. Then You will become a seven-day wonder. People will believe in You when they see such a spectacular feat!"

Temptation No. 3

"Is not the view breathtaking? Up on this mountain it is like being on top of the world. I will give You everything You can see. Just do one thing for me, Jesus. Kneel down in front of me, and worship me. It is as simple as that." They were all very real satanic attacks. But "after the devil left Jesus, angels came and helped Him." (See Matthew 4:1–11.)

The devil and Jesus' betrayer

When Jesus' best friend, John, wrote about Judas Iscariot betraying Jesus, he used these words: "The devil had already put into his heart the thought of betraying Jesus." (See John 13:2.) When Jesus chose Judas as one of His 12 apostles, He said, "One of you is a devil!" (See John 6:70.)

Jesus calls Peter "Satan"

Jesus told His disciples, "In Jerusalem, I will be put to death." Peter thought he knew better: "Far be it from You, Lord. This shall not happen to You!" Jesus did not mince His words. In His reply He called Peter "Satan": "Get behind Me, Satan! Your thoughts do not come from God." (See Matthew 16:21–28.)

"Your father is the devil"

The Pharisees did not just argue against Jesus. They wanted Jesus dead—all the while pretending that they were oh, so religious! Jesus told them a truth about themselves: "You are the children of your father, the devil. He is a murderer and a liar." (See John 8:42–47.)

16 ASSORTED FRIENDS OF JESUS

A foreign woman

It was not done. Rabbis and teachers would not be caught dead talking to women in public—let alone to a Samaritan woman, a woman of a despised race. Yet Jesus had a long talk with her by a well. When Jesus' disciples saw this, "they were greatly surprised to find Jesus talking to a woman." (See John 4:1–42.)

The one person who said thanks to Jesus

Jesus healed ten people from the dreadful skin disease of leprosy. Only one came back to Jesus. He fell on his knees and said, "Thank You." He was a foreigner, a hated Samaritan. Jesus was so pleased with him that He said, "Get up, and go. Your faith has made you well." (See Luke 17:11–19.)

People who did not have much education

We do not have a record of many of Jesus' prayers. But in one we do have, we see how happy Jesus is that you do not have to be greatly educated to be His follower. Jesus prayed, "Thank You, Father, that You have shown to the unlearned what You have hidden from the learned and wise." (See Matthew 11:25.)

The man nobody would go near

Being a person with leprosy made you an untouchable. If such a person walked down the street, everyone scattered. So when a man with leprosy came up to Jesus, he was amazed by what Jesus did. Jesus loved him, had compassion on him, spoke to him, touched him, and healed him. (See Mark 1:40–45.)

The blind man who was made an outcast

Jesus healed a man who had been blind from birth. As usual the healing did not please the Pharisees. They questioned the healed man as if he were a criminal. They were fed up that the man would not speak badly about Jesus, and furious that he spoke up for Jesus: "One thing I know: I was blind, and now I see." So, "they threw him out of the synagogue." (See John 9:1–41.)

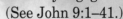

The woman who was about to be stoned to death

Caught in the act! "Here she is," said the Pharisees. "We caught her committing a sin. Should not she be stoned to death?" Jesus replied, "He who is without sin among you, let him throw a stone at her first." They all slinked away, starting with the oldest. Jesus had reassuring words for the woman: "I do not condemn you. Go and sin no more." (See John 8:1–11.)

A beggar

We don't even know the name of this beggar. He was in a dreadful state. He was poor and blind. He was begging as usual in the main street of Jericho as Jesus passed by on His way to Jerusalem. "Jesus, Son of David, have mercy on me!" the beggar called out. Jesus stopped, called him, asked him what he wanted, and healed his blindness. The sighted beggar then followed Jesus, praising God.
(See Luke 18:35–43.)

17 EIGHT PROMISES OF JESUS

The promise about Jesus making life great

Some people think Jesus is a spoilsport. The opposite is the truth. Jesus said, "I have come that you might have life, and that you may have it more abundantly."
(See John 10:10.)

The promise about Jesus giving His life for us

Jesus was quite clear about why He died. He did not die to show how good He was at enduring physical pain and verbal abuse. He "came to give His life to redeem many people."
(See Mark 10:45.)

The promise about those who give things up for God

Jesus never promised an easy life for His followers. But He did say that it would be well worth it. Jesus said, "I tell you that anyone who leaves home or brothers or sisters or father or mother or children or lands, for My sake and the gospel's, will receive much more in this time. …and in the age to come, eternal life."
(See Mark 10:28–31.)

The promise about Jesus coming alive again

When Jesus rose from the dead, all His followers were taken by surprise. But Jesus had told them many times that was how it would be. Jesus told His disciples plainly, "I will be put to death, but three days later I will be raised to life."
(See Matthew 16:21.)

The promise about Jesus never leaving His followers

Jesus' last words appear in the final verses of the last chapter of Matthew's gospel. Jesus promises to stay with His disciples always: "I am with you always, even to the end of the age." (See Matthew 28:16–20.)

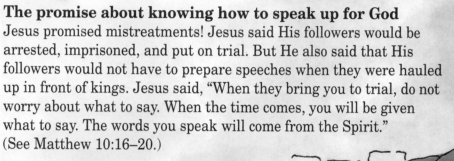

The promise about knowing how to speak up for God

Jesus promised mistreatments! Jesus said His followers would be arrested, imprisoned, and put on trial. But He also said that His followers would not have to prepare speeches when they were hauled up in front of kings. Jesus said, "When they bring you to trial, do not worry about what to say. When the time comes, you will be given what to say. The words you speak will come from the Spirit." (See Matthew 10:16–20.)

The promise about Jesus coming back to earth

Jesus said that He would one day return to earth. Then it would not be as a helpless baby but as King of kings and Lord of lords. When Jesus ascended to heaven, His followers were told, "This Jesus, who was taken up from you into heaven, will come back in the same way as you saw Him go into heaven." (See Acts 1:1–11.)

The promise about life in heaven

Jesus prepared His followers for the time when He would no longer be with them. He told them not to be worried or upset because He would return and take them to be with Him—in heaven. (See John 14:1–4.)

18 SEVEN PEOPLE JESUS HEALED

The man who had been ill for 38 years

Just imagine it. Being ill and unable to walk for 38 years. When Jesus saw the man who was unable to move, He said to him, "Get up, pick up your mat, and walk." At once, the man did all three things.
(See John 5:1–18.)

Jairus's 12-year-old daughter

"Talitha, cumi!" These are Jesus' actual words. They mean, "Little girl, I tell you to stand up." The words stuck in people's minds. It was such an odd thing to say to a dead girl! But all of a sudden she was not dead. She was standing up and walking around. "Give her something to eat," Jesus said to her surprised parents.
(See Mark 5:22–24, 35–43.)

The mother of the wife of Peter

Jesus did not heal only strangers. Peter's mother-in-law had a fever. Jesus went straight to her bedside, took her by the hand, helped her out of bed—and she was fit as a fiddle.
(See Mark 1:29–31.)

The boy with an evil spirit

The boy's father explained it all to Jesus. His son was in a really bad way. "Whenever the spirit attacks him, it throws him to the ground, and he foams at the mouth, grits his teeth, and becomes stiff all over." Jesus saw it for Himself: "The boy fell on the ground and rolled around, foaming at the mouth." With these words, Jesus cured the boy: "Deaf and dumb spirit, I command you, come out of the boy and never go into him again!"
 (See Mark 9:14–29.)

A man who could not hear or speak

"EPHPHATHA!" That was the actual word Jesus used when He met a man who could not hear or speak. The word means, "Open up." Jesus "put His fingers in the man's ears, spat, and touched the man's tongue." And he was cured. Little wonder that everyone was completely amazed: "He makes both the deaf to hear and the mute to speak!"
(See Mark 7:31–37.)

The woman who could not stand up straight

For 18 long years the unfortunate woman could not stand up straight: "She was bent over and could in no way raise herself up." Jesus placed His hands on her, and at once she straightened herself up and praised God.
(See Luke 13:10–17.)

The man who had dropsy

Edema is the medical name for the man's illness. Swollen arms and legs, especially swollen ankles, were the telltale signs. While the Pharisees pulled their beards and held a religious discussion about healing on the Sabbath, Jesus did the healing. He healed the man of his illness. (See Luke 14:1–6.)

19 JESUS AND FATHER GOD

He is My Father

Jesus was under fire: "You are only a Man, but You are trying to make Yourself God!" How would Jesus reply? Jesus had a double-barreled response. God was His Father and He was united to Him: "The Father is in Me, and I am in the Father." You cannot get closer than that.
(See John 10:38.)

Abba

When Jesus prayed to His heavenly Father, He called Him "Daddy." He said, "Abba, Father." Jesus was so close to His Father that He thought of Him as His loving dad.
(See Mark 14:36.)

He sends rain on everyone

Here is a thought for a rainy day! Everyone in the world may not love God, but God loves everyone in the world. Jesus said, "Your Father in heaven makes the sun to shine on bad and good people alike, and gives rain to those who do good and to those who do evil."
(See Matthew 5:45.)

He is a God of love

What is God like? You can tell a lot about God from His actions and what He has done. The most famous verse in the Bible says, "God is a God of love." This is John 3:16: "For God so loved the world that He gave His only begotten Son, that whoever believes in Him should not perish but have everlasting life."

He will send the Spirit

When Jesus left His disciples, He promised them that the Holy Spirit would replace Him. Jesus said that "the Father" would give us the Holy Spirit to be our Helper and Comforter and Guide.
(See John 14:16–17.)

We are a team

Jesus is part of a three-person team—the Father, the Son, and the Holy Spirit. Jesus once said to His Father, "All I have is Yours, and all You have is Mine. You and I are one."
(See John 17:6–19.)

**You have seen Me;
you have seen Him**
"If only I could see God, then I
would believe," has been the
boast of many. Well, Jesus came
to show us what God is like.
Jesus even said, "Look at Me
and you have seen God." Jesus
told His disciple Philip,
"Whoever has seen Me has seen
the Father."
(See John 14:8–14.)

20 SEVEN WAYS OF THINKING ABOUT JESUS

Jesus is like a good shepherd

A shepherd had to protect his sheep against bears and lions. A good shepherd was even prepared to die for his sheep. So people knew what Jesus meant when He said, "I am the good shepherd, who is willing to die for His sheep." (See John 10:11.)

Jesus is like a vine

Ripe juicy grapes hanging on vines are a common sight in Israel. So Jesus said, "I am the vine, and you are the branches. Whoever remains in Me, and I in Him, will bear much fruit; for without Me you can do nothing." It is so obvious. Break off a branch from a tree and it dies. Jesus says, Stay close to Me, or you will die.
(See John 15:1–10.)

Jesus is the way to God

Billy Graham loves to use this quotation at his Crusades: "I am the way, the truth, and the life." In huge letters this sign is put up. The rest of the quote is: "No one comes to the Father except through Me."
(See John 14:6.)

Jesus is like bread

Bread is the everyday food for most people. It feeds us, nourishes us, and keeps us going. In a spiritual way this is what Jesus does, and so He said, "I am the bread of life. He who comes to Me will never be hungry."
(See John 6:35.)

Jesus is the light of the world

In Jesus' day, like today, people walked in darkness, sadness, poverty, misery, and hatred. Jesus said, "I am the light of the world. Whoever follows Me will not walk in darkness, but will have the light of life." (See John 8:12.)

Jesus is like a door

At night a shepherd built a circular wall from stones. He would leave one gap in the circle so he could drive the sheep in. Then to keep them safe, he would lie down and go to sleep across this gap. In this way he was a "door," a way in and out for the sheep. That is why Jesus said, "I am the door of the sheep." (See John 10:7.)

Jesus is the resurrection and the life

"I am the resurrection and the life. He who believes in Me, though he may die, he will live." This is said at nearly every Christian funeral service. Followers of Jesus believe that when we die, our bodies may be dead and buried, but our spirits are alive with Jesus in heaven. (See John 11:17–27.)

21 NAMES JESUS WAS CALLED

He was crazy
The Pharisees said about Jesus, "We are certain You have a demon." This is what the top religious leaders thought of Jesus: "You are crazy!" (See John 8:48.)

The Son of God
It was the tough-as-nails army officer who called Jesus by this name. He had just watched Jesus die on the cross and said, "Truly this Man was the Son of God!" (See Mark 15:39.)

The Lamb of God
John the Baptist saw Jesus coming toward him. He wanted to let everyone around him know who Jesus was. So John said, "There is the Lamb of God." Lambs were used in the Old Testament as a sacrifice for sins. To make sure everyone remembered this, John added, "…who takes away the sin of the world!" (See John 1:29.)

Jesus
Mary and Joseph did not choose the name for their "miracle" baby. No, an angel told Joseph in a dream what His name should be: "You will name Him Jesus." The angel went on to explain the meaning of this name, "Because He will save His people from their sins." (See Matthew 1:21.)

22 HOW DID JESUS PRAY?

By Himself
Before special moments in His life, Jesus often went off by Himself to pray. He found the hills particularly peaceful. Jesus could pray all night long. (See Luke 6:12.)

With His friends
Jesus did not always pray by Himself. Jesus once took His three closest friends, Peter, James, and John, with Him to pray. As usual, He went to a hillside. That was the time when Jesus was transformed before their eyes, which is now called the Transfiguration. (See Luke 9:28–36.)

He asked God to bless His friends
When Jesus prayed for His disciples, it is very interesting to see exactly what He prayed for. He prayed, "Keep them safe." How could this happen? "By the power of Your name" (*name* meant "who you are"). Safe from what? "Safe from the the devil." (See John 17.)

The Jesus prayer (part two)

Whereas the first part is all about God, the second part is all about the things we need, and we are to pray for them:

"Give us this day our daily bread.
And forgive us our debts,
As we forgive our debtors.
And do not lead us into temptation,
but deliver us from the evil one."

(See Matthew 6:7–13.)

Pray for those who mistreat you

Jesus taught His disciples that they were not to take revenge on people, not even on those who mistreated them. The disciples were to pray for them. Jesus said, "Love your enemies, and pray for those who persecute you."
(See Matthew 5:44.)

In a garden

The garden was called Gethsemane, the Garden of the Olives (Gethsemane means "oil press"). It is still there today, outside the walls of Jerusalem, full of olive trees. Just before Jesus was arrested He went there to pray.
(See Matthew 26:36–46.)

The Jesus prayer (part one)

Jesus left us a model prayer. Jesus said, "When you pray, this is how you should pray:

Our Father in heaven,
Hallowed be Your name.
Your kingdom come.
Your will be done on earth as it is in heaven."

23 JESUS' LAST WEEK

Sunday

Jesus rode humbly into Jerusalem on a donkey. A conquering king would have charged in on a war horse. As Jesus arrived the crowds cut down palm branches and spread them on the road. They shouted, "God bless Him who comes in the name of the Lord! Praise God!"
(See Matthew 21:1–11.)

Monday

Jesus cleared the temple. Jesus found the Court of the Gentiles full of traders. The money changers were making massive profits as they exchanged money. Jesus drove them out and overturned their tables.
(See Matthew 21:12–17.)

Tuesday

For a lot of this day the Pharisees argued against Jesus. "What right have You to do these things?" they angrily protested. On this day Jesus also likened Himself to a mother hen looking after her little chirping chicks.
(See Matthew 21:23—24:51.)

Thursday

(Nothing is mentioned about what happened on Wednesday.) Thursday was the day of the Last Supper. In secret Jesus celebrated the Passover with His 12 disciples. We call this day Maundy Thursday because during the meal Jesus said, "I give you a new commandment" (John 13:34). The English word *Maundy* comes from the Latin word *mandatum*, which means "commandment."

Friday: flogged
Judas betrayed Jesus. Jesus had to go through an illegal trial. Pontius Pilate had Him whipped, and the soldiers mocked Him and pressed a crown of thorns on His head. (See Mark 15:15–20.)

Friday: cross carried
Pilate sentenced Jesus to death. The soldiers forced a passerby, Simon from Cyrene, to carry Jesus' cross, following behind Jesus. (See Luke 23:26.)

Friday: the nails
Jesus was crucified with two criminals. One was on His right, and one was on His left. Being nailed to the cross and tied with cords and then left to die on the raised cross was the most painful death anyone has ever had to go through. Sometimes this lingering death could take days. One person took nine days to die. (See Luke 23:32–34.)

24 JESUS' LAST MEAL

Washing feet
Actions speak louder than words. Jesus wanted to teach His disciples an important lesson: "You should wash each other's feet." So Jesus acted like a servant and washed their feet. Certainly they never expected that! (See John 13:1–17.)

A prediction
Jesus made this prediction: "The Scripture must come true that says, 'He who eats bread with Me has turned against Me.'" Eleven of the disciples did not know what Jesus meant. So Jesus said plainly, "One of you will betray Me." (See John 13:18–21.)

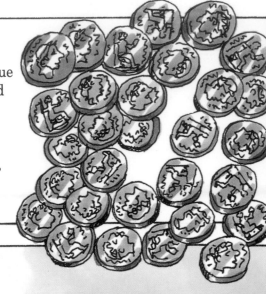

"Who is it, Lord?"
The disciples were completely puzzled about what Jesus meant. Peter whispered to John, "Ask Jesus who He is talking about." So John asked Jesus, "Who is it, Lord?" Jesus answered, "I will dip some bread in the sauce and give it to him. He is the man." (See John 13:22–26.)

Exit Judas
Jesus took a piece of bread, dipped it, and "gave it to Judas Iscariot, the son of Simon." John records this very sad moment: "Judas accepted the bread and went out at once. It was night." It was not only dark outside. It was dark in Judas's soul. (See John 13:26–30.)

Bread
"As they were eating, Jesus took a piece of bread, gave a prayer of thanks, broke it, and gave it to His disciples. 'Take and eat it,' He said. 'This is My body.'" We now call this the Lord's Supper, or the service of Holy Communion.
(See Matthew 26:26.)

Wine
"Then Jesus took the cup, gave thanks to God, and gave it to them. 'Drink from it, all of you,' He said. 'This is My blood, poured out for the forgiveness of sins.'" The bread was Jesus' body, and Jesus said the wine represented His blood. Jesus said, "Do this in remembrance of Me."
(See Matthew 26:27–28; Luke 22:19.)

The Mount of Olives
After the Last Supper they sang a hymn, probably from Psalms 115, 116, 117, or 118. (The Psalms were their hymnbook.) Jesus then went to one of His favorite places for prayer. He went to the Mount of Olives.
(See Matthew 26:30.)

25 JESUS ON TRIAL

Judas betrays Jesus with a kiss

A kiss is a sign of special friendship. Matthew records this: "The betrayer had given the crowd a signal: 'The Man I kiss is the One you want. Arrest Him!' Judas went straight up to Jesus and kissed Him."
(See Matthew 26:47–56.)

From Annas to Caiaphas

Annas sent Jesus to his son-in-law, Caiaphas, who was the high priest that year, for a second unfair trial. Try as they might they could not find Jesus guilty of anything. They even had their own witnesses give false evidence, telling all kinds of lies about Jesus.
(See Matthew 26:57–67.)

Jesus goes to Annas

Soldiers and religious officials arrested Jesus in the Garden of Gethsemane. They tied up His hands and took Him off to Annas, who had once been high priest.
(See John 18:12–14.)

First visit to Pontius Pilate

Jesus was then taken from the religious court, the Sanhedrin, to Pilate, the Roman governor of Judea. The people did not like Pilate, but only Pilate could pass a death sentence. Pilate disappointed the people because he declared, "I find no fault in this Man."
(See Luke 23:1–5.)

King Herod meets Jesus

Pilate sent Jesus to Herod. Herod was in charge of Galilee, but he was in Jerusalem then. Herod looked forward to seeing Jesus. He hoped to see Him perform a miracle. Jesus disappointed Herod. He did not answer one of Herod's questions, let alone do a miracle. Fed up, "Herod and his soldiers treated Jesus with contempt and mocked Him. Then they put a fine robe on Him, and sent Him back to Pilate." (See Luke 23:6–12.)

Pilate sets Barabbas free

Pilate made a feeble attempt to release Jesus. But he ended up freeing Barabbas, a convicted criminal on death row. (See Matthew 27:15–26.)

The death sentence

"The crowd chanted, 'Crucify Him! Crucify Him!' They demanded with loud voices that Jesus be crucified. And finally their shouts succeeded. Pilate handed Jesus over to them to do as they requested." (See Luke 23:21–26.)

26 THE DAY JESUS DIED

The notice in three languages

If you had looked at the top of Jesus' cross you would have spotted a notice that the other two crosses did not have. Pilate had written, "Jesus of Nazareth, the King of the Jews." To make sure everyone who passed by could read it, it was written in three languages, Greek, Latin, and Hebrew.
(See John 19:19–22.)

Gambling for Jesus' clothes

After the Roman soldiers had crucified Jesus they sat down and had a game of dice. The prize for the winner was Jesus' clothes.
(See Mark 15:24.)

Come down if You are God

Even when Jesus was in agony on the cross, "the chief priests and the teachers of the Law and the elders mocked Him: 'He saved others, but He cannot save Himself! If He comes down off the cross now, we will believe Him.'"
(See Matthew 27:41–43.)

The dark noon

"It was about noon when the sun stopped shining, and there was darkness over all the earth until three o'clock." Then Jesus died. Although we call it Good Friday, it was a very dark day.
(See Luke 23:44.)

People around the cross

Many of Jesus' most faithful followers were women. They watched Him, with great love in their hearts, as He was on the cross. "Among them were Mary Magdalene, Mary the mother of James and Joseph, and the wife of Zebedee." Also there were Mary, Jesus' mother, an aunt of Jesus, and the wife of Clopas. (See Matthew 27:56.)

The temple curtain torn

The moment after Jesus died, the great curtain in the temple was torn in half from top to bottom. The great curtain had separated the Holy of Holies from the people. The torn curtain showed that Jesus' death opened up the way to God. (See Matthew 27:51.)

The earthquake

After Jesus died "the earth quaked, and the rocks were split apart." (See Matthew 27:51–53.)

Scared soldiers

The tough, superfit Roman soldiers were reduced to masses of knee-shaking wobbly jelly. They were terrified by the earthquake. (See Matthew 27:54.)

27 JESUS' SEVEN WORDS FROM THE CROSS

Word No. 1

Jesus said seven things from the cross. These are sometimes known as Jesus' seven words from the cross. As the Roman soldiers banged the nails through His ankles and hands Jesus prayed, "Father, forgive them. They do not know what they are doing."
(See Luke 23:34.)

Word No. 2

To the dying criminal who asked Jesus to remember him, Jesus said, "I promise you that today you will be with Me in Paradise."
(See Luke 23:43.)

Word No. 3

"Jesus saw His mother and the disciple He loved standing by. He said to His mother, 'He is your son.' Then he said to the disciple, 'She is your mother.'" From then on the disciple, John, took Mary to live with him.
(See John 19:26–27.)

Word No. 4

Jesus told everyone that He felt that God had left Him. "At about three o'clock Jesus cried out with a loud voice, 'Eli, Eli, lama sabachthani?' which means, 'My God, My God, why did You abandon Me?'"
(See Matthew 27:46.)

Word No. 5

Just before Jesus died, He said, "I am thirsty." A sponge soaked in cheap wine was put on a stalk of hyssop and lifted up to Jesus' lips. Jesus drank it.
(See John 19:28–30.)

Word No. 6

Jesus' next to last word from the cross was a cry of triumph: "It is finished!" He had completed everything God sent Him to do.
(See John 19:30.)

Word No. 7

As Jesus gasped for air He took one big final breath and cried out in a loud voice, "Father, into Your hands I place My spirit!"
(See Luke 23:46.)

28 EVIDENCE FOR JESUS' COMING ALIVE AGAIN

Jesus really did die on the cross

You could not fool experienced Roman soldiers. They had broken the legs of the two men crucified with Jesus. But when they came to do the same to Jesus, they found Him already dead. "One of the soldiers pierced Jesus' side with a spear." (See John 19:31–34.)

Roman guards would have stopped any body thief

To steal the dead body of Jesus you would have had to be a superhuman. Roman soldiers were on guard. Pilate "gave orders for Jesus' tomb to be carefully guarded until the third day so that His disciples were not able to steal the body." (See Matthew 27:62–66.)

Why did Pilate not find Jesus' body?

If Jesus' coming alive again was not true His body would be lying in the tomb. All Pilate needed to do was find the dead body of Jesus. Then all talk of Jesus' being alive would be buried forever. But the one thing Pilate could not do was show the dead body of Jesus. (See Matthew 28:11–15.)

The cloth around Jesus' head: the clue

You need to be a detective here. Here is the clue. When John went into the tomb where Jesus' body had been put, he saw something that made him believe that Jesus was raised from the dead. He saw the burial cloth that had been around Jesus' head folded up.

The cloth around Jesus' head: the solution

Here is the solution to this puzzle. Seeing this folded cloth, John believed in Jesus' resurrection. Why? Because if you had been stealing a dead body you would not trouble to remove all the linen wrapping wound around it. You certainly would not fold up the head cloth all neat and tidy. You would steal it all. (See John 20:1–9.)

The soldiers saw it all

The soldiers saw an angel of the Lord, with dazzling clothes as white as snow, roll the stone away from Jesus' tomb. The soldiers were so scared they were like "dead men."
(See Matthew 28:1–4.)

The great cover-up

The soldiers rushed back to the chief priests and told them everything. One thing the chief priests were good at: quick thinking. "They gave a large sum of money to the soldiers and said, 'You are to say that His disciples came at night and stole Him while you were asleep.'"
(See Matthew 28:11–14.)

The disciples were changed

After Jesus died, before His disciples knew that He was alive, they met in secret behind locked doors. Once they saw Jesus alive they became fearless preachers. They happily, joyfully, endured beatings, imprisonments, and even death. Only Jesus' resurrection makes sense of this.

29 WITNESSES TO JESUS' RESURRECTION

The first person to the tomb

Mary Magdalene got a shock. Early on Sunday morning, while it was still dark, she went to the tomb and could not believe her eyes. The stone had been taken away from the entrance.
(See John 20:1–2.)

The first person into the empty tomb

Peter and John set off for the tomb together. John must have been the youngest, or at least the fittest, because he got there first. But he did not rush in. Peter dashed into the tomb as soon as he arrived, leaving John outside.

The second person into the empty tomb

John then followed Peter into the tomb. "He saw and believed." What did he see? "He saw the linen cloths lying there, and the handkerchief that had been around Jesus' head. It was not lying with the linen cloths, but folded together in a place by itself."
(See John 20:3–10.)

The first person to see Jesus alive

Mary Magdalene asked two angels where Jesus' body had been placed. Then Mary met the risen Jesus, although she did not recognize Him at first. But as soon as Jesus said her name, "Mary," she knew it was Jesus.
(See John 20:11–18.)

Ten disciples in a locked room

On Sunday evening 10 of Jesus' disciples, "afraid of the Jewish authorities," were having a secret meeting. Jesus came in through the locked door. His first reassuring words to them were, "Peace be with you." (See John 20:19–22.)

Seven disciples by Lake Tiberias

Peter, John, James, Nathanael, Thomas, and two other disciples had caught no fish all night. From the shore, unrecognized, the risen Jesus told them to throw the net on the right side of the boat. They caught 153 fish! Back on dry land, "none of the disciples dared ask Jesus, 'Who are You?' because they knew that it was the Lord." (See John 21:1–14.)

Ten disciples plus doubting Thomas

Exactly a week later, the risen Jesus met them in the same way. Jesus invited "doubting" Thomas, who must have been embarrassed, to do what he had asked: "Put your finger in My hands and your hand into My side." Thomas could only say, "My Lord and my God!" (See John 20:24–29.)

Over 500 people at once

Yes, a crowd of over 500 people saw the risen Lord Jesus. This is how the apostle Paul records the event: "Jesus was seen by more than five hundred of His followers at once." (See 1 Corinthians 15:1–7.)

Cleopas and a friend

A disciple of Jesus called Cleopas and a friend (whose name we do not know) were walking on the road from Jerusalem to Emmaus. Jesus joined them, but they did not have a clue who they were talking with. They were just about to start a meal together in Emmaus when "Jesus took the bread and said the blessing. Then He broke the bread and gave it to them." The eyes of the two were opened and they recognized Jesus. Then Jesus disappeared. (See Luke 24:13–35.)

30 THE FIRST CHRISTIANS

Matthias, the first reserve

Judas, who betrayed Jesus, had committed suicide. The apostles met to choose a replacement. He had to be someone who had been with Jesus when He was alive and who had witnessed a resurrection appearance of Jesus after His death. Joseph, called Barsabas, and Matthias were suggested. The apostles prayed and drew lots. Matthias was chosen.
(See Acts 1:12–26.)

Peter preaches: 3,000 say yes to Jesus

Peter preached to the crowds. It was exciting. All about Jesus. All about Jesus' resurrection. No less than 3,000 people believed.
(See Acts 2:14–41.)

The Holy Spirit arrives

Jesus had promised this would happen. The Holy Spirit came in dramatic style. There was a great noise, like a strong wind. They saw what looked like tongues of fire sitting on the disciples. And they all spoke their own languages. They were so full of joy that people thought they were drunk! Peter even had to say, "These people are not drunk!"
(See Acts 2:1–15.)

Arrested by King Herod

The grandson of the King Herod who was visited by the wise men was also called King Herod. He put Peter in prison. The night before Herod was going to execute him an angel rescued Peter. Some time later King Herod was parading himself around as if he were God Himself. God's angel struck him: "Herod was eaten by worms and died."
(See Acts 12.)

Prison and worse

Again, it was just as Jesus said it would be. The first followers of Jesus were put into prison and beaten. The first two Christian martyrs were Stephen and James. Stephen was stoned to death by a crowd of leading Jews, and James was killed with a sword on Herod's orders. (See Acts 7; 12:2.)

Saul falls off his horse

It was not just a riding accident. Saul was on his way to kill as many Christians in Damascus as he could. Suddenly he fell to the ground as a light flashed from the sky. He heard a voice: "Saul, Saul! Why are you mistreating Me?" "Who are You, Lord?" asked Saul. "I am Jesus," the voice said. (See Acts 9:1–19.)

Enemy to Christians turns into fearless preacher

Saul, an enemy to Christians, became Paul, the fearless preacher. Paul too suffered greatly as he traveled all over the known world telling everyone who would listen about Jesus and His resurrection. He said, "I have been in three shipwrecks and in danger from robbers. I have been whipped, I have been stoned, and once I was left for dead. Five times I was given the 39 lashes by the Jews." (See 2 Corinthians 11:23–29.)

The news about Jesus reaches Rome

The hub of the world in Paul's day was Rome. One of Paul's great ambitions was to preach about Jesus in Rome and to help the Christians in Rome. He fulfilled this ambition—but not quite in the way he had originally hoped. He arrived in Rome a prisoner, on trial for his life, because he was a Christian preacher. The last verses of the Acts of the Apostles picture Paul "for two years living in a rented house as a prisoner, teaching about the Lord Jesus Christ with all confidence." (See Acts 28:30–31.)